ALL
SORTS of
Shapes

For Stephen Dodd. E.D.

Picture Window Books
5115 Excelsior Boulevard
Suite 232
Minneapolis, MN 55416
877-845-8392
www.picturewindowbooks.com

Printed in the United States of America.
First published by Zero to Ten (a member of the Evans Publishing Group)
2A Portman Mansions, Chiltern Street, London W1U 6NR, United Kingdom

Library of Congress Cataloging-in-Publication Data

Reidy, Hannah.
All sorts of shapes / written by Hannah Reidy ; illustrated by Emma Dodd.
p. cm. – (All sort of things)
Summary: Compares a variety of objects to others with the same shape, such as bubbles and scoops of ice cream, bricks and ice cubes, and bicycle wheels and pizza.
ISBN 1-4048-1061-7 (hardcover)
[1. Shape–Fiction.] I. Dodd, Emma, 1969- ill. II. Title. III. Series.
PZ7.R27377Alss 2004
[E]–dc22   2004023876

ALL SORTS of Shapes

Written by Hannah Reidy

Illustrated by Emma Dodd

Special thanks to our reading consultant:
Susan Kesselring, M.A.
Literacy Educator
Rosemount-Apple Valley-Eagan (Minnesota) School District

PICTURE WINDOW BOOKS
Minneapolis, Minnesota

The bright paper pieces that Patrick and Penny are pasting

have four **corners,**
just like the pictures.

5

Just like the wheels
on the bikes
whizzing past,
Polly's pizza is
round and **flat**.

Corina's cake has three
pointy **corners.**

It looks just like the flag
on Phoebe's castle.

Steve's strawberry ice-cream scoops are as **round** as the bubbles Bonnie blows.

Justin likes cool **cubes** of ice in his juice.

They have **six sides,**
just like Vicky's bricks.

It's party time
at little Leo's.

There are lots of candles and **tall**, **thin** glasses.

Patsy loves pasta and
ice cream with ripples.
She prefers food
that **wiggles**
and **squiggles**.

Eat late in the evening,
by the light of the moon.
Curvy pieces of fruit
help to keep you cool.

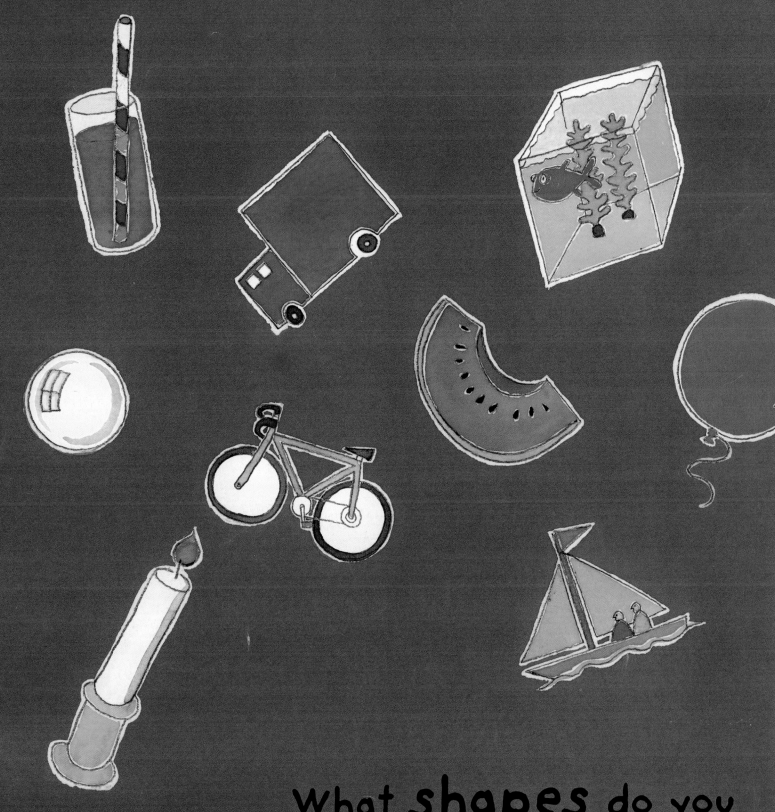

what **shapes** do you

think these are?

FUN FACTS

- A circle has no beginning and no end.

- Squares have four equal sides and four corners.

- Triangles have three sides and three corners.

- Curvy fruit is very good for you. Fruit is one of the five basic food groups.

WORDS TO KNOW

corners—the points where lines come together, like walls in a room

cubes—square blocks with six equal sides

curvy—lines that start to form circles; not a straight line

ripples—waves or ridges in something

round—the shape of a circle

whizzing—zipping by quickly

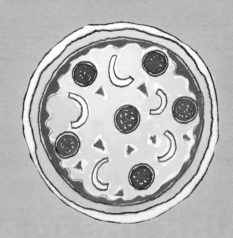

TO LEARN MORE

At the Library

Dodds, Dayle Ann. *The Shape of Things*. Cambridge, Mass.: Candlewick Press, 1994.

Hoban, Tana. *Shapes, Shapes, Shapes*. New York: Greenwillow Books, 1986.

Murphy, Chuck. *Shapes*. New York: Little Simon, 2001.

On the Web

FactHound offers a safe, fun way to find Web sites related to this book.

All of the sites on FactHound have been researched by our staff.

www.facthound.com

1. Visit the FactHound home page.

2. Enter a search word related to this book, or type in this special code: 1404810617

3. Click on the FETCH IT button.

Your trusty FactHound will fetch the best Web sites for you!

INDEX

Look for all of the books in the All Sorts of Things series:

All Sorts of Clothes

All Sorts of Noises

All Sorts of Numbers

All Sorts of Shapes